YOU ARE NOT ALONE

30-DAY DEVOTIONAL

Copyright © 2021 Latrice Mayes

ALL RIGHTS RESERVED. This book contains material protected under International and Federal Copyright Laws and Treaties. Any unauthorized reprint or use of this material is prohibited. No part of this book may be reproduced or transmitted in any form or by any means, electronic or mechanical, including photocopying, recording, or by any information storage and retrieval system without express written permission from the author/publisher.

Unless otherwise noted, all Scripture quotations are taken from the New International Version of the Bible. All rights reserved.

Scripture is taken from the New International Version®. Copyright © 1978 by Biblica. Used by permission. All rights reserved.

Book Cover Concept: Antwan M. Gardier

Book Cover Design: Prize Publishing House

Printed by: Prize Publishing House, LLC in the United States of America.

First printing edition 2021.

Prize Publishing House

P.O. Box 9856, Chesapeake, VA 23321

www.PrizePublishingHouse.com

ISBN (Paperback): 978-1-7371829-5-5

ISBN (E-Book): 978-1-7371829-6-2

The PEACE that you need

The JOY that you need

The LOVE that you need is in God....

You are not alone!!

Latrice Mayes

Dedication

To my husband, Lakil Mayes, I humbly want to say, "Thank You"! You have sacrificed so much to see me fulfill my God-given purpose, and for that, I am so grateful. You have been my rock, my listening ear; you have given me great ideas and allowed me to glean from your strength. You pushed me even when I wanted to give up and so much more. With all the tears that were shed, all the pain I endured, and all the opposition against me, you helped me overcome, and this book is dedicated to you! I love you with every fiber of my being.

To all of my children, I want to say, "Thank You"! Jowan, Marquell, Antwan, Ariel, Shamauri, and Amanti, you have been right there helping me along the way. A special shoutout to my youngest son, Antwan Gardier, for taking my idea and bringing it to reality for my book cover. It means a lot when you can depend on family to push you into greatness.

To my best friend, Sauna, who has stayed up on the phone many nights listening to my ideas and rants. You are such a great listener and friend to have right by my side. You helped me in more ways than you would ever know. "Thank You" so much!

Latrice Mayes
YOU ARE NOT ALONE: 30-DAY DEVOTIONAL

"Thank You" to all who have played a part in my life, from the only two pastors I have ever had to my family, friends, and even my enemies. The trials and opposition I have faced helped push me to write this 30-day devotional to help free every reader who reads it. Remember, you are not alone!

Introduction

Growing up, I experienced so much trauma that it left me in a broken and confused state of mind. I remember being angry, feeling lonely, feeling inadequate, going through an identity crisis, dealing with abusive men, and so on, living life every day as if I was okay. I started to think that was the norm because that is what I was use to seeing. I didn't realize that I could be free until one day I heard about the God that heals, the God that delivers, and the God that sets free and all that He had to offer.

See, people like you and I are born every day in this world full of sin in different families and raised differently, but somehow, we have to come to a place where we want change, and sometimes it has to begin with us. We go through life wondering who we are and why we are here. We often find ourselves asking the question, "Why Me."

Sometimes we find ourselves going through moments in life where we become suicidal, we try to fit in, we go through an identity crisis, we search out answers from the wrong people, and we end up going through the same thing over and over again. It then becomes a repeated cycle that keeps going and never stops. I have concluded that we must seek out the cycle breaker. The one who came to make us whole and complete, lacking nothing. The one who loves us unconditionally. The peace that we need, the joy that we need, and the love we need are all in God!

Once we realize who God is, we will be certain and confident in knowing that we are not alone. We may go through our ups and downs, but God always remains the same. In fact, Hebrews 13:8 states that Jesus Christ is the same yesterday, and today, and forever.

I pray this 30-day journey that you are about to embark on will enlighten your mind, inspire you to pick up the broken pieces, encourage you to muster up enough strength, and push you into greatness to fulfill your God-given purpose. Take the time to self-reflect and answer the questions so healing can take place. The first step to healing is admitting that there is a problem at hand. Go forth and be great!

Scripture of the Day!!

Jonah 1:3 – *"But Jonah ran away from the Lord and headed for Tarshish. He went down to Joppa, where he found a ship bound for that port. After paying the fare, he went aboard and sailed for Tarshish to flee from the Lord."*

Questions of the Day!!

How many times have you heard the voice of the Lord and turned a deaf ear?

_____
_____
_____
_____
_____

Do you hear GOD daily telling you to go one way, and you deliberately do the opposite?

_____
_____
_____

_____

_____

_____

Inspiration of the Day!!

Life has a way of pushing us all in every direction, whether for good or bad. Somedays, we may find ourselves doing things and saying things we know are not in God's will. I am not talking about cursing, fighting, or stealing but plain ole being disobedient.

Something as simple as the Lord telling us to encourage someone we don't particularly care for. While we are trying to decipher which way to go, we should not go without Jesus leading us. When the Lord leads us, we do not have to worry, be afraid, or be fearful because He is all-wise and all-knowing, and He will lead us in all truth.

When God speaks to us, we must incline our ears and hearts to hear and receive. Everything that comes from the mouth of God is always beneficial and will always help us grow along the way. See, Jonah became angry with God! He knew God was very gracious and compassionate towards His people. God sent Jonah to deliver a word to a sinful city called Nineveh. Instead of being obedient, he chose to flee far away from God. In his fleeing, Jonah caused a great storm to arise. The only way the storm ceased was when he was thrown overboard in the sea.

Can I leave you with this? Submitting to God will make life so much easier! What do you do when God calls you for such a task, and you feel unequipped, uneasy, and unprepared? Will you trust Him to lead you, or will you run as Jonah did?

Testimonial......

God called me at an early age, but because of my lack of understanding and the fact that I loved the life I was living, I kept living in sin. I was prophesied to at the age of 16 and ran. Again, at 18 and many times after that, I brushed it off because I didn't understand. One thing I came to realize, we can flee when God calls our name, but when He wants our attention, He has a way of getting it and keeping it.

God blessed me to become pregnant with a baby boy in 2003, and on April 1, 2004, I gave birth to a 5 lb. 5oz. son who was stillborn. I was devastated and did not know who to turn to. What I did know was that I needed help! I was not strong in my faith, did not come from a spiritual background, and did not know much about God, but I had heard of Him. I was in a very dark place! I stopped eating. I was not sleeping. I was heartbroken. I had to go to many doctor's appointments. I still had four other children and a husband that craved my attention. I was diagnosed with gestational diabetes, and so on and so on. I had so much going on emotionally and physically that it seriously affected my mind and body.

You know what that did! It turned my face to the God that I had heard about. I wanted to see if what I heard about God was true. It bought me closer to God because I knew that in the mindset I was in, nobody else could help me. After praying and seeking God, I began to ask Him why this had to happen and what He wanted me to get out of it. I began to pray and ask God to show me my son. He did all that I asked and more! See, God is the giver of life, and He has every right to take what He gives when He wants to. Again, He knows how to get our attention and keep it. When God calls, pick up the phone and answer. Yes, sometimes it is hard to pick up our bed and walk with God, but it will be all worth it in the end.

Scripture of the Day!!

Psalms 27: 10 – *"When my father and my mother forsake me, then the Lord will take me up."*

Questions of the Day!!

Who are you allowing to occupy your time during your brokenness?

_____
_____
_____
_____
_____

While feeling deserted, what are you spending most of your time doing?

_____
_____

_____

_____

_____

_____

Inspiration of the Day!!

Growing up, I always had questions in the back of my mind about my father because he was never around. As I grew, I heard things like he was in and out of jail, he has a substance abuse issue, and he fights a lot, but none of that really matters as a child. All you ever want as a little girl is to be daddy's little girl. So many other things used to go through my head, such as: why did he abandon me, was I not good enough, does he love me, etc., and believe it or not, those thoughts stuck with me in my adult years.

After fully giving my life to Christ and studying His word, I realized Psalm 27 was speaking directly to me. When we feel abandoned, alone, hopeless, broken, and desolate all we must do is reflect on God's word. The Lord will take me up speaks volumes!!! When the Lord holds us close to Him, He will teach us how to love ourselves, to know who we are, and to whom we belong.

In life, the normal people to look to for help would be our parents (the person who raised us), but what if we cannot lean on them? What if they do not want to be bothered with us? God knows who is for us and who is against us, and regardless of the person, we must pray and ask God for clarity and understanding. We all have a purpose, and maybe the person God removed was not part of His plan. I prayed out of desperation to God because I just did not understand, and this is what he revealed to me……

Vision from God……

I was at a wedding, and at the end of the wedding, we started to exit the building. The bride, another woman, and I were walking down a dark street, and then we came to a house full of people. As the bride went into the house, I stared at the door because I could see a man that looked just like my daddy. As the man started walking toward the door, he hugged everyone he could before he walked out. The closer he got, I could see more clearly, and I started walking down the street to get away from him. He came out of the house and saw me, and began to walk toward me. When he got closer, he asked me for a hug, and I told him no two times, and he began to get angry.

By this time, the bride came down to where we were, and she had a baby on her hip. My dad asked her if he could hold the baby. He turned the baby sideways and began to throw the baby's head toward my head. After that, I stood up and told him I would give him a hug to keep him from hurting the baby. He spoke to me and said to me that if I would have hugged him, I could have prevented what happened and told me I would have damage to the left side of my brain.

What was God telling me? He spoke to me and said I was protecting you from dangers that could have taken root in you. I am all-wise and all-knowing, and because I know the plans for your life, I altered it. See, sometimes we can't see past our own emotions, but God knows what to do and when to do it.

✦✦✦ Day 3 ✦✦✦

Scripture of the Day!!

2 Corinthians 3:17 – *"Where the spirit of the Lord is, there is liberty."*

Questions of the Day!!

What stronghold are you allowing to keep you in bondage?

_____
_____
_____
_____
_____
_____

What is keeping you up at night?

_____
_____
_____

_____

_____

_____

Inspiration of the Day!!

Being in quarantine, we had a lot of free time to ourselves. We had to get adjusted to the new norm. Our daily lives (daily routines) have been altered in some shape, form, or fashion. The normal going to church, having family gatherings, date night, going to work has all come to a stop. What are we going to do now?

Can I suggest to you that in a season where everything seems to be altered, we should conform with the change and keep going, keep pushing, keep praying, keep reading our word, and keep submitting ourselves to God? During this quarantine, our lives have only been altered temporarily, but that does not mean that our relationship with God should be altered. In fact, being in this place has lightened up the load of our daily schedules (we have a lot of free time) to get closer to God. Remember, the things that we need God to break in our lives can only be done through a relationship with Him. The strongholds, generational curses, sicknesses, brokenness, bitterness, and everything that has attached itself to us from our childhood (through our family lineage) to now can only be destroyed through our relationship with God. God does not want us to walk around in bondage. He wants us to be free. In fact, He came that we may have life and have it more abundantly. As we go throughout our day, we must set aside some time for our creator, redeemer, strength, and first love. We all are coming out victorious and better than we were before if we take God at His word. The first step to breaking chains off our lives and being free is decreeing and declaring.

Affirmation......

- Generational curses are broken off my family.
- I shall live and not die.
- Sickness, illness, and disease no longer reside in my body.
- My unsaved love ones are saved.
- My household is blessed.
- I have more than enough.
- My marriage will strive, thrive, and survive.
- My bank account is overflowing.
- I am covered under the blood of Jesus.
- Chains are being broken and destroyed off my life, my children's lives, and my family's lives.
- I am free.
- _____
- _____

- _____
- _____
- _____
- _____

✦•✦ Day 4 ✦•✦

Scripture of the Day!!

Ephesians 3:17 – *"That Christ may dwell in your hearts by faith; that ye, being rooted and grounded in love."*

Questions of the Day!!

Does Jesus still have the deed to your heart?

_____
_____
_____
_____
_____

Does Jesus still occupy space within?

_____
_____
_____

_____

_____

_____

Inspiration of the Day!!

If we are not watchful and careful daily, it is so easy for something to creep up and take residence in our hearts. God reveals who He is from within, so we must have Him in our hearts to be able to understand in the spiritual realm. Having Christ on the inside of us is what helps us maintain a holy and righteous life. Everything that we need is in Christ! The joy that we need, the peace that we need, the strength that we need, and the love we need all come from the Lord. Even the voids that we may have can only be filled by Jesus Christ.

When we give up our will to take on the will of our father (Jesus Christ), He will teach us, guide us, and lead us in all truth. One thing I have learned in my years of living is that whatever is in our heart is what we are going to give most of our time to and entertain. In this day and time, social media is popular. Being on electronics has become the new norm. Watching TV and listening to music has taken over, and it is all good for a while, but don't allow it to reside and occupy the place where Jesus lodges. Sometimes we must make ourselves uncomfortable and get out of doing things the traditional way. It will bring discomfort and pain, but it will be beneficial to us in the end.

Testimonial......

In my early years of serving Christ, I was not as strong as I would have liked. Just to give you a little background of how I used to be! I was raised in the projects (Lincoln Park) fighting, cursing, bad attitude, etc., so I was always ready. I found myself being one way at home and another way around my family. Receiving calls to fight, cursing folks out without hesitation, and fornicating was the norm for me, all while still going to church.

As I gained strength from Christ through fasting, praying, and reading my Word, I also had to pull away from my family. I realized that until I got to the place where I am not tempted by my weakness, I had to stay in a place where I could gain strength from God. I really wanted a deeper, more intimate relationship with Christ, so I had to do what I had to do. Trying to understand God fully and desiring for Him to lodge in my heart, I knew that I could not half-step. I had to give God my entire heart!

See, I was the one family and friends would call because I was the bold one. With me separating myself, I decided where I was going, when I was going, how long I would be there, and what I would give my attention and time to. It was a choice I had to make!

Sometimes we must stand still and wait on God. We must stand still until God equips us with what we need. We must stand still until we have gained enough strength to be able to face our weaknesses and not be tempted. It was hard because we are a close family, but it had to be done.

Latrice Mayes
YOU ARE NOT ALONE: 30-DAY DEVOTIONAL

God recognizes the heart, and when we are pure and ready, He will meet us where we are. We must come to a place where we want God more than the desires of our flesh.

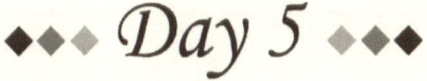

Scripture of the Day!!

Matthew 19:26 – *"But Jesus beheld them, and said unto them, with men this is impossible; but with God all things are possible."*

Questions of the Day!!

Who are you allowing to discern (watch) over you?

_____

_____

_____

_____

_____

_____

Who are you allowing to speak over your life?

_____

_____

_____

_____

_____

_____

Inspiration of the Day!!

Have you ever been in a situation in life where you felt like it was going to be an epic failure? With your natural eye, you just didn't see a way out. You looked to your family; you turned to your friends; you even talked it over with your pastor, and still NO relief. Then you realize Matthew 19:26 fits your situation, so you decide to have a little talk with Jesus. See, man has limited resources and access, but God has unlimited resources. Everything we need, everything we want, everything that we desire is in God.

What does the word impossible mean? According to the New Oxford American Dictionary, it means not able to occur, exist, or be done. In English terms, it can't be done by man's hand! Man doesn't have the power nor the resources to accomplish what needs to be done. We must learn how to trust God with every part of our being, especially for the things that can't be done with man's abilities. So many times, we go before God and try to fix things off of our own abilities and strength, not realizing that we can't fix it. Remember, in all things if it is impossible to man, it is definitely possible with God. Give it to Him and allow Him to keep it. Don't you dare take it back!

Testimonial......

When I first started being in a committed relationship, I didn't know a thing about marriage. All of the pain, the hiccups, the selflessness, the communication, the sacrifices, and all that comes with marriage can be very challenging at times. My husband and I started dating at a young age. I was 19, and he was 22, and when you are that young, you are ignorant to the devil's tactics.

I learned to be wise and aware of the enemy's schemes. I learned to speak life over every situation that looked dead. I learned to keep people (outsiders) out of my relationship. See, I knew he was the one, but I wasn't sure if we would make it because of the lack of an example of how to love, submit, and cherish my husband. When we realize we have something good and don't want to lose it, we start fighting for what we want.

After years of fighting with the devil and against my relationship, I decided to give my life to Christ. After receiving Christ, He taught me how to be a wife, a mother, loving, submissive, willing to listen, and sensitive to my husband's feelings. Although my husband had his own issues, I had to go to God for myself. Sometimes the change starts with us! Keep in mind He didn't teach me how to argue, fuss, and fight, nor did He teach me how to change my husband. This was something God had to work out in me.

After years of allowing God to break me down so He could build me back up, I started to see a change in my marriage.

A lot of times, we go into marriages thinking we can change the other person when that's not our job to do. Our job is to live the life that God put before us so that they can see the change. A few scriptures helped me get through the rough patches in my marriage, and after 22 years together, we are happy and going strong. God can work out everything that seems impossible to man. A few scriptures to meditate on that helped me with my marriage:

- Proverbs 15:1 – "A soft answer turneth away wrath: but grievous words stir up anger."

- Ephesians 4:32 – "And be ye kind one to another, tenderhearted, forgiving one another, even as God for Christ's sake has forgiven you."

- Galatians 5:22-23 – "But the fruit of the spirit is love, joy, peace, longsuffering, gentleness, goodness, faith, meekness, temperance: against such, there is no law."

- Proverbs 14:1 – "Every wise woman buildeth her house: but the foolish plucketh it down with her hands."

You Are Not Alone!!!

◆◆◆ Day 6 ◆◆◆

Scripture of the Day!!

Joshua 1:5 – *"There shall any man be able to stand before thee all the days of thy life; as I was with Moses, so I will be with thee: I will not fail thee, nor forsake thee."*

Questions of the Day!!

Do you know that you are never alone?

_____
_____
_____
_____
_____

Do you know who is with you every step of the way?

_____
_____

_____

_____

_____

_____

Inspiration of the Day!!

God is with us! God is a keeper of His word and His promises. God has made a covenant in His word that He will never leave us nor forsake us (which means He will never desert nor abandon us). He is always there, but by any chance, we don't feel Him near its not because He left us, but we have left Him. God loves us so much that He is willing to go that extra mile to make sure that we experience that Agape love. He will show us dreams and visions to warn us. He will reveal things to us in the supernatural. He will allow us to see things and hear things, etc., just to warn us about the things happening around us.

Why do you think God is so adamant about letting us know He is with us? I believe that God called us out because He has a purpose and a plan for our life. Could it also be God is so adamant about letting us know that He is with us because He doesn't want us to feel alone? Could it be that God knows we can't make it without Him? Could it be God has work for us to do? Could it be that God needs us to minister to the lost souls that only we are assigned to? Could it be God put something in us that nobody else possesses? Whatever the reason, we must remember that what God has for us to do is tailor-made just for us, and nobody else can do it. We don't ever have to feel like we are in this thing called life alone because God is always with us. He is fighting for us, He is going before us, and He is working things out on our behalf. God is not like man; He will not fail us!

Vision......

My family and I were at a gas station, and a young lady came towards my daughter and tried to harm her. When I wouldn't let that happen and attempted to defuse the situation, the little girl went home to get her mom. When she left, I could hear people talking, saying things like her mom is crazy, she has guns, she is going to come back up here and start something, etc. As I walked back into the store, the lady at the counter asked if I wanted to see the surveillance cameras (look to see what really happened). After watching the video, I walked outside, and the young lady and her mom were outside. The young lady walks up to my daughter and tries to fight her again, and her mother is yelling in the background, urging them to fight. I stood up and told them no one was fighting! I told my daughter to run, and as she was running, the lady took a gun out of her car and started shooting at my daughter. I started running to get away from the lady, and every time she would shoot the gun, the bullets would never touch us. The scripture that came to mind was Ephesians 6: 16 when it talks about quenching the fiery darts of the wicked. God is our protector, and He will do just that, protect us. Don't worry about the plots and plans that the enemy is storing up for us because our God is a restorer, and He will give us just what we need to stand. The most amazing thing to me is we are not standing by ourselves, but He is right there, standing with us. #NEVERALONE #HEISALWAYSWITHME #JUSTWHENINEEDHIMMOSTHESTEPSRIGHTIN

❖❖❖ Day 7 ❖❖❖

Scripture of the Day!!

Matthews 7:15 – *"Beware of false prophets, which come to you in sheep's clothing, but inwardly they are ravening wolves…."*

Questions of the Day!!

Do you know the company that you keep (who is in your circle)?

_____

_____

_____

_____

_____

_____

Who are you?

_____

_____

_____

_____

_____

_____

Inspiration of the Day!!

To discern who we have in your circle, we must first do a self-examination to find out who we are. So many times, we become friends with the enemy unknowingly.

Growing up, I used to hear the saying, we attract who/what we are. Once we learn who we are and seek God, we will become wiser when choosing our friends. In this day and time, we have something that we call counterfeit friends, they look one way on the outside, but their motives are totally different on the inside. These wolves talk like us, dress like us, sit by us, work with us, go to church with us, and sometimes they are even put in positions over us. One must be as wise as a serpent and harmless as a dove! It is so easy for a counterfeit to blend in with the original because it shares many of the same qualities. Having people in our circle can be detrimental when we don't know who they are, who sent them, and why they are there.

Many people don't know, but sometimes people are sent to attach themselves to us for a season to drain the life out of us. The fact that the word of God is warning us about false prophets indicates that they are out there lurking. They are looking for that one who is vulnerable, weak, and has their guard down. We must be watchful, prayerful, discern who we have in our circle, and know who we are as a person. In all things, we must seek God for wisdom and discernment so we won't be blindsided. The people in our circle should push us into greatness, inspire us to be better, encourage us to fulfill our purpose, and love us unconditionally with no strings attached. They should be able to see the best in us even when we don't see it in ourselves.

I want to leave you with this!! Please don't downplay your anointing and gifts trying to fit in with those that were not sent by God. They are the very ones that need you to stand because they need what you have to make it. God only made one of you (nobody else can be you, do you, or replicate you), so be the best you.

Vision……

I was in bed sleeping, and as I went to step out of bed, I looked to the right, and I saw a wolf standing at my door in my room. I started to get up and walk towards the door in fear because I knew it was abnormal for a wolf to be at my door. As I am walking toward the wolf, it sits down and stares at me. I shut the door and preceded to clean my room. I then go to another room to clean, and when I looked back, the wolf started to run after me. I ran into the other room, and as I was shutting the door, I peeked out, and it was sitting at the door. Again, I began to clean that room as well.

The funny thing in the vision was the wolf's characteristics were totally opposite of its nature. When I awakened, I heard Matthews 7:15 clearly. God revealed to me that I needed to clean up my circle and be watchful in this season of my life. Everybody is not equipped or purposed to be attached to you in this season. The only way we will know is through God. It is imperative to know who we have in our personal circle in this season of our lives. Be aware!!

❖❖❖ Day 8 ❖❖❖

Scripture of the Day!!

Romans 8:28 – *"And we know that all things work together for good to them that love God, who are called according to his purpose."*

Questions of the Day!!

Did you know that you were called out from among the majority?

_____
_____
_____
_____
_____

Do you know everything that you have been through in your life will work out for your good?

_____
_____

_____
_____
_____
_____

Name one thing that you went through and thought was going to take you out!

_____
_____
_____
_____
_____

Inspiration of the Day!!

What we go through in life doesn't always feel good to us, but it always works out for the good when we trust God. Storms that we endure in life can sometimes cause depression, stress, complacency, bitterness, worry, doubt, suicidal thoughts, and so on but God being all-wise and all-knowing, knows how to come in and deliver. It is in those days that we must learn how to put whatever we learned into action.

The Lord allows us to go through different experiences not to destroy us but to build character, develop a more intimate relationship, help us trust Him more, and have a oneness with Him. If we are honest, many of us wouldn't be where we are today if something detrimental would not have knocked on our front door. God knows what process He must allow us to go through to get our attention and sometimes to push us into our God-given purpose.

Sometimes we look at sicknesses, pain, discomfort, brokenness, heartache, etc. as a bad thing, but in reality, they are the things that push us to pray, they are the things to cause us to seek after God's heart, they are the things that keep us on our knees praying to God.

We were called to do a great work for the Lord, and as I stated before, He has to get our attention because we are called. Ladies and Gents, molestation/rape, brokenness, generational curses, sickness, abandonment, and everything we had to encounter were not meant to take us out. Dust yourself off, get back in the game, and fight for your life. It will be worth it!

Testimonial......

November 14, 2019, is a day that I will never forget. It was a night that my family and I had to pull on God in more ways than one. I stayed up the night before preparing/packing to go on a women's retreat that I was so excited to attend. As my husband and I were getting ready for bed, he dropped to his knees and held his head in excruciating pain. He told me it felt as if somebody was hitting him in the back of the head with a hammer. He then stated to me that he needed to go to the hospital, so I called the ambulance, all while praying. While we were waiting for help, so much took place. He started vomiting everywhere. He fell in the kitchen and eventually became incoherent. When we got to the hospital, we found out that he had a brain aneurysm and had to have emergency surgery.

The hospital stay was very hard at first! I had to watch my husband on a ventilator the first day. He had a tube draining out of his head for about two weeks, and he was bedridden for about two weeks. My load was easier when I heard the Lord speak to me and said, make this room your personal sanctuary, and the rest was history. My husband and I started listening to uplifting music, watching inspirational messages, praying together, and that is what bought us through.

After spending almost a month in the hospital (without any physical therapy, speech therapy, nor occupational therapy), he was released. That is what serving God will do for us. We may go through the storm, but God will make sure that we are equipped to weather it. My husband's hospital stay has caused him to have a closer walk with God and gave him a new perspective on life. He prays more, reads his word more, and has his one-on-one time with God. Because of his hospital stay, God has birthed "Women Who Slay" (serve, love, anointed, yearn for Christ). He has birthed a conference, "911 Emergency Help is on the Way", this book you are reading (*You Are Not Alone*), and other ministries that are forthcoming. Don't look at what you are going through as the end! It's just the beginning of something new.

♦♦♦ Day 9 ♦♦♦

Scripture of the Day!!

1 Corinthians 16:10-12 – *"Again, Jesse made seven of his sons to pass before Samuel. And Samuel said unto Jesse, the Lord hath not chosen these. And Samuel said unto Jesse, Are here all thy children? And he said, there remained yet the youngest, and behold he keepeth the sheep. And Samuel said unto Jesse, send and fetch him: for we will not sit down till he come hither. And he sent, and brought him in. Now he was ruddy, and withal of a beautiful countenance, and godly to look to. And the Lord said, arise, anoint him: for this is he."*

Questions of the Day!!

Have you ever felt overlooked?

_____
_____
_____
_____
_____

Have you ever been in a place where you didn't feel like you were good enough?

_____

_____

_____

_____

_____

Inspiration of the Day!!

A lot of times, we operate out of emotions because that is what we are used to. We sometimes allow the opinions of others to dictate who we are, what we should look like, and where we are going. In reality, the only person who should be able to dictate how our life turns out is God. In 1 Corinthians, I can only imagine how David felt when all of his other brothers were bought before Samuel, and he was left in the field to tend to the sheep. I can also imagine the stench he must have had on him from being outside with those animals. In life, we don't know what the end of the road will look like. We can feel underqualified, not good enough, overlooked, etc., but when God qualifies us, all of the other things go out the door.

We can worry about what people think or what people may say. Trust God, trust His plan, trust His purpose for your life! When we put our trust in Him, He will exalt us in due season. He will bring us before great men. He will elevate us. Don't worry about where you are at this point in your life. Again, when we trust God, everything will fall into place! Please don't look at where you came from, where you have been, what you did, or who you did. God doesn't call the qualified; He qualifies the called. DON'T SIKE YOURSELF OUT OF YOUR ELEVATION!!! It's yours for the asking.

Testimonial......

I decided to attend nursing school after delivering a stillborn baby boy. I wanted to make a difference in healthcare by showing true genuine love and compassion. After taking my prerequisites, I applied for the nursing program. I was accepted in the 1st cohort (1st thirty-two people), which was awesome. When I first started nursing school, I was sometimes looked over because of my skin color and judged by my outer appearance. We would go to clinicals, and I will hear things like, "I don't want her to be my nurse because she doesn't have blonde hair and blue eyes" or "Don't allow that nurse to come back in here because she doesn't look like me."

As time went on, I had professors that didn't want to help me learn. In my second year of nursing school, I had a professor change my grade and tried to fail me because of her own selfish reasons. She sent emails telling me she wasn't going to change my grades back. I remember coming home talking to my husband about it. I then prayed and went to sleep.

I had a vision that night about me going to the Dean of Nursing and talking to her about what went on. Everything that the Lord showed me in the vision (even the clothes the Dean had on) came to pass, and everything was taken care of. She ended up changing my grade to a "B," and I passed my class.

What am I trying to say? People may not like us, but they can't stop nor block us with God on our side.

Day 10

Scripture of the Day!!

Psalm 46:1 – *"God is our refuge and our strength, a very present help in the time of trouble."*

Questions of the Day!!!

What are you relying on for strength?

_____
_____
_____
_____
_____
_____

Who do you run to in the time of trouble?

_____
_____
_____

_____

_____

_____

Inspiration of the Day!!

Being born in the flesh, the Bible states in Job 14:1 that a man born of a woman is of few days and full of trouble. Having a carnal or righteous mindset, we sometimes think that we know what's best for ourselves and our situations. We seek how we can change our situations by operating off of temporary emotions (how we feel), only to find ourselves going in circles and finding ourselves in the same place where we started.

When we can't figure out the solution to our problem, we get on the phone and dial up momma, sister, cousin, and friend to find ourselves seeking ungodly counsel and in the same situation we were in before we made the phone call. In the time of trouble, we must know who we can run to for relief. From the time we made our grand entrance into this world until the day we take our final resting place to meet Jesus, we will endure many things in this life. Some things we endure we may bring upon ourselves, and other things happen because they were tailor-made just for us, but nevertheless, God will meet us where we are.

On a personal note, I know how life has a way of leading us down the wrong paths without knowing the right direction to go. Our past has a way of trying to creep up in our present without any warning. Why is it trying to show up? It's trying to show up to throw us off focus and cause us to go astray. As we grow in Christ, we realize that we can't make it off our own strength. When we face the troubles of this world, we can find rest in God, for He is our refuge and strength. No matter the trouble we may find ourselves in, God promised us that He would never leave us nor forsake us. He assured us that He would be with us even in troubling times.

So, when we are going through, we must know that we are not alone and we don't have to face our troubles by ourselves. God is our refuge, so rest in Him today and every day, knowing that He will protect us, keep us, and cover us. Again, rest in Him! God is our resting place.

Affirmation......

R - relax

E - ease your mind

S - submit to His will

T - trust Him fully

The JOY That You Need!!

◆◆◆ Day 11 ◆◆◆

Scripture of the Day!!

Psalms 139:14 – *"I will praise thee; for I am fearfully and wonderfully made: marvelous are thy works, and that my soul knoweth right well...."*

Questions of the Day!!

Do you accept the person you see in the mirror every day?

_____
_____
_____
_____
_____
_____

Do you know the way you look was purposely and carefully designed for you?

_____
_____

_____

_____

_____

_____

Inspiration of the Day!!

Living this thing called life sometimes can cause us to lose focus of who we really are and who we were designed to be. That can be both spiritually and physically! We look at different types of TV shows, read magazines, watch YouTube, look to our mentors, listen, and look at others to try and find our place in life. If we would be honest with ourselves, we sometimes find ourselves trying to mimic or live our lives through someone else. That's not how God intended for our lives to be. We were all formed in the image of God! Before we were formed in our mother's womb, God created the details of us inside and out. He created something from nothing so we could be unique and one of a kind in every area of our lives. From conception to delivery to birth, God orchestrated every part of our being so we can stand apart from everybody else.

In life, as we mature, we sometimes lose ourselves in being a spouse, a parent, working, going to school, working in ministry, etc. Even in the midst of losing oneself physically, we must muster up enough in us to know who we are. We are "FEARFULLY AND WONDERFULLY MADE," so we must learn to embrace who God has made us inside and out.

Look yourself in the mirror and do daily affirmations and speak over who you are. It doesn't matter your skin tone, how many moles and skin tags you have, the color of your hair and eyes, the shape of your body, the movement of your curves; you are exclusive. Death and life are in the power of your tongue, so speak over yourself daily. These are just a few you can speak over yourself. Feel free to add more….

Affirmations……

- ✓ I am beautiful!
- ✓ I am fearfully and wonderfully made!
- ✓ I love everything about me!
- ✓ I am the daughter of a King!
- ✓ I am royalty!
- ✓ I am confident in who God made me!
- ✓ I can do all things through Christ that strengthens me!
- ✓ I am who God said I am!
- ✓ I know my identity!
- ✓ I am fulfilling my God-given purpose!
- ✓ I know my self-worth!
- ✓ I am embracing the woman that I am!

- ✓ I am a virtuous woman!
- ✓ I am becoming the best me!
- ✓ _____
- ✓ _____
- ✓ _____
- ✓ _____
- ✓ _____
- ✓ _____

❖❖❖ Day 12 ❖❖❖

Scripture of the Day!!

Isaiah 41:10 – *"Fear thou not, for I am with thee; do not be dismayed; for I am thy God: I will strengthen thee; yea, I will help thee; yea, I will uphold thee with the right hand of my righteousness."*

Questions of the Day!!

Have you ever been through something, and you felt like you were all alone and had no one to turn to?

_____

_____

_____

_____

_____

_____

Can you name one thing that you are/were fearful of?

_____

_____

_____

_____

_____

Inspiration of the Day!!

Fear is not of God! Fear is of the devil, and it comes to distract and hinder us from moving forward in God. In fact, God has not given us the spirit of fear; but of power, and of love, and of a sound mind (2 Timothy). We can overcome every fear that the enemy tries to send our way. God has fully equipped us with power, strength, and endurance to defeat fear. Sometimes you have to look fear square in the eyes and speak to it. Don't allow fear to tell you who you are and what you can't do. We must learn to speak to fear and let it know that we are more than conquerors; we are fearfully and wonderfully made, we can do all things through Christ that strengthens us, we are who God says we are. God has given His children (born-again believers) tools to conquer.

Three things that we can do to overcome fear:

1. We can overcome fear with **PRAYER**
2. We can overcome fear with **POWER** (The Holy Ghost)
3. We can overcome fear with **THE WORD OF GOD**

In times when fear tries to come and overtake our minds, we just have to face it. Life and death are in the power of the tongue, so we can speak to it and send it back to where it came from. Don't allow fear to lodge or take residence in your spirit. Once we allow fear to take root within us, we begin to take on the spirit of being complacent and stagnant, which means we will stop growing. Why? Fear will paralyze us and cause us to experience anxiety, panic attacks, breathing difficulty, and so much more. We have to make sure that we are allowing God to lead us and regulate our emotions. Remember, in the midst of any storm that we are experiencing now, we can speak to it and command it to go. Let's start on today decreeing and declaring the word of God in the midst of whatever it is we are facing on today. Fill in the blank lines, and let's make this personal!

Affirmation......

- ✓ I am healed_____
- ✓ I am more than a conqueror_____
- ✓ I am fearfully and wonderfully made_____
- ✓ I am delivered_____

- ✓ I am free_____
- ✓ I am strong_____
- ✓ I can make it_____
- ✓ I am an overcomer_____
- ✓ I am more than enough_____
- ✓ I am blessed_____
- ✓ I am saved_____
- ✓ I am strong and courageous_____

Day 13

Scripture of the Day!!

Psalm 30:2 - "O Lord my God, I cried unto thee, and thou hast healed me."

Questions of the Day!!

Have you ever had a sickness, illness, or disease that you were dealing with that you needed to be delivered from?

_____
_____
_____
_____
_____

Have you ever been desperate for a touch from God?

_____
_____

_____

_____

_____

_____

Inspiration of the Day!!

A few years ago, I went to a women's retreat to be revived, rejuvenated, and encouraged to keep pushing. After a full, long day of eating, playing games, shopping, and being poured into, me and a few women went back to our room to shower, relax, and get ready for the next day. During the women's retreat, earlier that day, a young woman spoke about breast cancer and gave us pamphlets and information to read at our leisure.

While preparing for bed, I took a shower and decided to check my breast for a lump or anything unusual. My heart dropped when I realized that I found a lump. Going through the rest of the weekend with the ladies, I didn't say a word. After I got home, I made an appointment with my doctor to get it checked out, which led to her sending me to a specialist. When I visited the specialist, he instructed me that I would need to have surgery to check and see if it was benign.

God visited me one day in my dream and let me know everything was going to be okay. The details of the dream are below!! See, when we face opposition in our bodies, we need to go to the creator of the body—the one who can perform surgery with no surgical team and heal with no medications. I won't dare tell you that I didn't get scared, that I didn't cry, that I didn't question what God was doing, but through it all, I learned how to regain focus and trust God. In my years of seeking God, I have learned how one will know God as a healer if He (God) never healed you. We can testify and help others with empathy if we have been through it. Whatever has attached itself to you, unwanted and uninvited, and you are looking for God to heal you, I have four words "Cry out to Him." He loves you and hears your cry! You don't have to suffer from any sickness, illness, or disease when serving the master healer.

Dream......

God showed me in one of my friend's church sanctuary sitting down in about the 3rd row, watching a preacher encourage his flock. My friend and I were just sitting there looking and listening to the word, and as the preacher was preaching, a shout broke out in the church. One of the young ladies who was shouting grabbed my arm and asked me to get up and shout with her. As I proceeded to get out of my seat and step into the church aisle, I started running. When I woke up out of the dream, I was encouraged to know that the words spoken in the dream were there to uplift/encourage me. Can I tell you later on that week I received a phone call from this friend asking me to go to church with her and the rest was history? When we got there, I was in the same area where I was in the dream, and the preacher was up giving an encouraging word. He then called a prayer line and asked everyone who desired prayer to come up as he anointed his hands with oil. When I went up there, he laid hands on me and preceded to tell me what the Lord said. In the midst of him speaking, he instructed me to take my hands and push away from myself to get rid of everything trying to afflict my body. I praised God in the aisle and in my seat. I went to have surgery, had the lump removed, and it was benign. Can you shout our God is a HEALER! See, it doesn't matter what the situation looks like. What does matter is that we win at the end when we trust God.

❖❖❖ Day 14 ❖❖❖

Scripture of the Day!!

Jeremiah 1:5 – *"Before I formed thee in the belly, I knew thee; and before thou camest forth out of the womb I sanctified and I ordained thee a prophet to the nations."*

Questions of the Day!!

Will you spend the rest of your life trying to please others (trying to fit in)?

_____
_____
_____
_____
_____

Will you allow how others see you to define who you are?

_____
_____

_____

_____

_____

_____

Inspiration of the Day!!

To know what we are in God, we must first know who we are. Many of us go through life without knowing who we are because we have answered to what others have called us or spoken over us. Sometimes God reveals to us who we are, but life has a way of making us forget who God called us to be. I want you to know that you are an exception to the rule. God created you to be a **SPECIAL CASE**! We no longer have to walk around wondering who we are, what God called us to be, if we are in the right place where God wants us, etc. God provides everything that we desire to know in His word. We have been through so many things that could have taken us out of here, such as car accidents, bad divorces, being overlooked in ministry, sicknesses, loss of jobs, being evicted, and so on, but look at us. We are still standing. Why? Everything that we have endured, God kept a special covering over us to protect us. When we were born, God called us and sanctified us for His purpose and His plan. As you are reading this, I want you to know that you are not your past. Today, look these things in the face and tell them you no longer have control over me. If I didn't come down your row write down on the lines provided the things you need to say goodbye to.

- Depression
- Suicidal thoughts
- Spirit of torment
- Fornication/Adultery
- Fear
- Discouragement
- Generational curses
- _____
- _____
- _____

Being the exception, we have access to things that others don't have access to. Remember God called us! Whom God calls, He also qualifies. Trust God! We are not who the world says we are. We are everything that God says we are.

Testimonial......

I always knew that I was different from the masses. Once I realized that being different does not always mean it's bad, I overcame a lot. Even though I knew God called me, I didn't know who I was in God. I tried to depend on man to help me figure out who I was in the kingdom and my assignment. After several failed attempts and walking away discouraged, I decided that I was just going to give up because I just didn't understand. Lack of wisdom and understanding left me in a vulnerable state of mind, and I knew after a while I needed to be freed to fulfill my purpose.

Sometimes God has to strip us away from man's opinion so that we can hear His voice clearly. What man doesn't fully understand can't be properly articulated! God formed us, God knows us, and God called us, so what better source can we turn to than to Him. We have to come to a place in our life where we stop looking for man's approval and stop dummying down our anointing to fit in.

Are we going to make people upset by flowing in your anointing? Yes! Will some people treat us differently? Yes! God called us all to do a work in the kingdom, and it can't be done out of fear, living in our past, going through an identity crisis, not being aware, etc. We must stand up and know that we are the exception to the rule, and because we are the exception, God is there to lead and guide us into all truth. Remember, we are not who man says we are, but we are everything God says we are!! You are qualified for what God called you to, and you will fulfill your purpose and kingdom assignment!

◆•◆ Day 15 ◆•◆

Scripture of the Day!!

Proverbs 22:6 – *"Train up a child in the way that they should go: and when they are old, he will not depart from it."*

Questions of the Day!!

What path are you leading your children down?

_____
_____
_____
_____
_____
_____

What has been planted in your children that will grow over time?

_____
_____

_____

_____

_____

_____

Inspiration of the Day!!

In this day and time, we have to be connected to the all-wise, all-knowing, and all-around omnipresent God. Raising children can be a challenge all by itself, but with the help of the Lord, He will lead/guide us. Being connected to God is essential and imperative to raising children today so that His word can be embedded in them. We never know what plots the enemy has set up for our children (youth), but if they are raised on a firm foundation (the word of God), they will always revert to God. Even though they may stray away after their own lust and lifestyles, they won't forget the teachings about God, the Sundays we took them to church, the songs they sang in the choir, and the time we spent reiterating the word of God. When the right things are instilled in them, the temptation will come, and they may fall off the wagon, but they will always know where their strength comes from. What was taught to them will not leave them. How do I know? My husband and I raised six children who are now 25, 24, 23, 19, 18, and 14, and though it has been a challenge, it has also been a blessing. Raising them was an honor and blessing from the Lord. God favored us, and I took it to heart because God entrusted us with their little lives, and the least we can do is raise them in His word. You know it's God when none of your children have been in trouble with the law, all but the youngest was working while in school, none of them have behavior problems, none of them been suspended from school, all of them graduated high school, and so on. Training them up in the right way really makes a difference in how they will turn out.

Dream......

My oldest daughter had a boyfriend that she would talk to daily. In their time together, they would talk like normal couples would. One day I was awakened by a dream that God showed me about her and the young man having a conversation. I heard their entire conversation about plans they were making and trying to leave my husband and I out of the loop.

In the vision, I saw my daughter and her friend discussing things that a mother wouldn't want to hear, and when I woke up, I was a little disturbed. Apparently, the vision I saw was on my face because when I walked out of my bedroom into the kitchen, she was washing dishes, and she asked, "Why do you look like that, mom?" I tried to get myself together because I wanted to seek God about it. I prayed and sought the Lord about it because I wanted to approach the situation in a non-judgmental way and humbly.

After talking, her facial expression told me before she spoke that it was true. She admitted that everything that God revealed to me was true, and she was embarrassed. God also spoke to her and convicted her heart and used her to interpret part of the dream. When we talked later that day, she just kept looking at me, wondering how God showed me their plans. God loves us all, and He has a plan for us, but sometimes because of immaturity, being blinded by the lust of our flesh, and plain out disobedience, we miss His voice, so He has to use someone else. Parents, if you don't know God and are trying to raise children on your own, I encourage you to get to know Him. Serving God, I promise, you will always be a couple of steps before your children.

The PEACE That You Need!!

✦✦✦ Day 16 ✦✦✦

Scripture of the Day!!

Romans: 26-27 – *"Likewise the spirit also helpeth our infirmities: for we know not what we should pray for as we ought: but the spirit itself maketh intercession for us with groaning which cannot be uttered."*

Questions of the Day!!

Do you know who is interceding on your behalf when you can't pray for yourself?

_____

_____

_____

_____

_____

_____

Is the spirit that you are connected to able to war (pray) on your behalf without you opening your mouth?

_____

_____

_____

_____

_____

Inspiration of the Day!!

It amazes me when I think about the God that we serve. A lot of times, we meet people, and they offer words of encouragement and even offer prayer to us. Some will pray for us openly, while others will tell us I am praying for you (we never hear them utter a prayer out of their mouth). When we are going through different situations in our lives, we need to be surrounded by those who are unashamed and bold to pray for us and with us.

There are times in our lives where we feel like we are covered and buried, and we need to be resurrected. We have stayed before God in prayer, fasting, seeking His will for our lives, studying His word, and sometimes can't find the words to pray for ourselves. Depression has taken over; stress has become the new norm; the lust of the flesh has overtaken the will to do what's right, and so on. I want you to know that even when you can't find the words to pray, the spirit makes intercession for you. When we find ourselves at our lowest low and feel like all hell is breaking out in our lives, the spirit is interceding for us. So, please remember when we are facing custody battles, grief, marital issues, financial hardships, are emotionally drained, etc., and feel like we can't get a prayer through Jesus is interceding for us.

Dream......

I was in my house in my room cleaning up. My oldest daughter, Ariel, was outside playing, and she ran to my window, calling my name. When I looked out the window, I saw a white cloud forming in the sky. It looked a little weird, so I went to the back door to see what was going on, and out of the cloud came an angel. It was amazing to look upon! The head looked like it was in the sky, and the feet looked as if they were on the ground. The angel stared at me with this big gigantic book in its hand and started talking to me about what was going on in my life. He looks at me all while he looks through the book, calling off names that are already written in the book. He then states to me what I had to do if I want my name to be written in the book. The angel reassured me that God was with me and that He would help me.

Day 17

Scripture of the Day!!

Genesis 16:13 – *"And she called the name of the Lord that spake unto her, Thou God seest me: for she said, Have I also here looked after him that seeth me......"*

Questions of the Day!!

Who do you call on in your time of despair (need)?

_____

_____

_____

_____

_____

Can you see the beauty that God sees in you?

_____

_____

_____

_____

_____

_____

Inspiration of the Day!!

When we were born into this world, we didn't have the choice to choose our own families, our genetics, our outer appearance, what to endure, or anything that pertains to this life. Over the years, I have learned and understood that as a people of this world, we tend to gravitate towards the things that we have learned from childhood to adulthood, and sometimes that can be conflicting/contradicting to God's word. As we grow and mature mentally, spiritually, and physically, we learn who we are and who we can call upon for help and who we can't. We must seek out God for those who are assigned to us in different seasons of our lives. Everyone is not graced to handle the anointing and oil that we carry, so we have to be strategic and connected to God so that He can reveal to us the hidden things. When God starts to reveal things to us in the spirit realm, we must seek out His face for clarity and understanding.

It is imperative to seek out the creator, the alpha, the omega, where it all starts and where it ends. Often we don't even see ourselves the way God sees us, which can be a distraction that will prolong what the Lord wants to do in us. Even though finding ourselves in Christ and learning to hear His voice can be challenging, staying focused and faithful produces fruitful results. When God speaks, we must incline our heart to His voice. We must not allow anything nor anyone to silence our voice.

Even in the midst of affliction, God can change the ending of our story. It doesn't matter where we came from, what we look like, how we look at ourselves; all that matters is that when God calls, we answer. When you don't understand, stay on the wall (in prayer) until you get an answer. God still answers prayers!!

Dream......

I had a dream on Jan. 9th that I was at a locker, and it was a lock that had numbers on it. In the dream, I heard the number 0406, and I could actually see them almost floating. As I began to turn the numbers in the lock and pull the lock to see if it was open, it was still locked. I felt the spirit of frustration, wondering why God would give me a dream and give me numbers to a lock and it not open. Toward the end of the dream, I heard a still voice speak to me and let me know that in due time it will unlock and to trust His timing.

On April 6 (0406) of the same year, I was awakened by someone sending me a video to watch at 5:00 in the morning. As I started watching it, I could feel the spirit of God as I was seeing walking canes and wheelchairs being hung up and people getting delivered. A few hours later, I had to leave and take my youngest daughter to school. As I was driving, the Lord spoke to me and said, look at the message that was sent. I looked at it again but couldn't understand what the Lord was saying to me. God spoke again and told me to look at the message, but this time I looked at the date and everything in between, and that's when I saw the number 0406. God spoke to me and said, this is the day that I am releasing your prophetic gift. From that particular day to now, I have been operating in the prophetic and strong.

♦•♦ Day 18 ♦•♦

Scripture of the Day!!

Psalms 37:4 – "Delight thyself also in the Lord; and he shall give thee the desires of thine heart. 5 Commit thy ways unto the Lord; trust also in him; and he shall bring it to pass."

Questions of the Day!!

Who are you committed to in this season of your life?

_____

_____

_____

_____

_____

_____

Who are you putting your trust in?

_____

_____

Inspiration of the Day!!

We find ourselves committing to relationships, jobs, friendships, ministries, material things, and everything under the sun that our fleshly desires have led us to. In the beginning, things were great, but as time passed, we realized this is not what God had ordained for our lives. Friendships start to fall off, relationships begin to fall apart, jobs go on a firing spree, and we find ourselves back at square one in need. We start losing things close and dear to our hearts, and we commit ourselves to the wrong people and the wrong things.

When we commit ourselves to the Lord and delight ourselves in Him, He promised to give us the desires of our hearts in His word. He **will not** go back on His word!! I went through a season in my life, and I felt like I lost everything from a child to my house and everything that's in it. That's why this scripture is dear to my heart because when we make up in our mind to trust the Lord, commit our ways to His ways, and delight ourselves in Him, He will give us our heart's desires.

Testimonial……

Our house was shot up over 100 times, and a bullet grazed my head. There were holes in my bedroom set, TVs, children's bedroom furniture, vehicle, etc. When we left our home that we owned, we left with one TV, our clothes, a computer/printer, washer/dryer, stove, refrigerator, and our lives. When I tell you, losing almost everything and trying to keep the faith was hard.

I am here to attest that it can be done with the help of the Lord. I want to let you know that as of today, we are in the process of purchasing another home, our entire house we stay in is fully furnished with brand new items and paid off (furniture and appliances), and we are debt-free. The Lord also saw fit to take us from having one car to now having two cars. He literally gave us double for our trouble, and we are here to testify about it. It is imperative to trust God with our entire being. Sometimes trusting Him can be very challenging but yet rewarding.

◆◆◆ Day 19 ◆◆◆

Scripture of the Day!!

2 Corinthians 6:14 – *"Be ye not unequally yoked together with unbelievers: for what fellowship hath righteousness with unrighteousness? And what communion hath light with darkness?"*

Questions of the Day!!

Are those you are connected to aligned with your purpose in life?

_____

_____

_____

_____

_____

_____

Do you really know who you are yoked with?

_____

_____

_____

_____

_____

Inspiration of the Day!!

Being in a relationship should be something we all look forward to as we grow and mature. Unfortunately, we sometimes look for what we lack or miss within ourselves, causing us to be yoked with people who were not aligned with our purpose. If we can be honest, some of us have linked up with individuals who have caused some kind of toxicity that causes us to bleed on others because of emotional attachments. Sometimes we have to face these attachments head-on and call them by name so deliverance can come and so we can walk in liberty. Abusive relationships, self-sabotaging, wanting to fit in, being broken, holding on to guilt, being misused, childhood pain, etc., are a few examples that cause us to link up with the wrong people.

I'm not promising you every day will be peaches and cream, but when you are in the will of God, He will fulfill His promises. Don't worry if you find yourself in this situation now or have experienced it before because God is our strong tower. God is our redeemer! God is our healer! Whatever we stand in need of God will supply. I want to encourage you to allow God to mend all the broken pieces of your life. When He mends them, it will all work out for your good. When desiring a relationship, allow God to bring the right one across your path. If you are yoked, blessing upon blessing will be upon your relationship because you are aligned with God's word. Again, it won't be perfect, but it will be blessed! Don't settle for less by allowing yourself to downplay what you deserve but allow God to bring the right one in your life that was tailor-made just for you.

Testimonial......

Growing up out the projects, you were counted out! You were stereotyped, and people thought you would either be a drug dealer, have several children with several baby daddies, abuse the welfare system, live in housing, etc. I have nothing negative to say because sometimes we need the system as a stepping stone to get on our feet.

Nevertheless, growing up, I felt alone and broken. I can count on one hand how many times I saw my dad. My mom was partying enjoying her best life, so it left me outback. I remember I started dating at 15 because I wanted to feel loved, and at 16, I got pregnant with my first child. I had my second child at 17. I was 18 years old with two children, and my children's father was incarcerated.

I remember taking the city bus from home to daycare and then walking to work Monday-Friday. It was tough, but I had to take care of my children. When I turned 19, I was introduced to this sweet young man who was almost five years older than me. That is my husband to this day. I am not going to lie! I have been hurt so much in my life that I really didn't want to be bothered because I thought he would hurt me too. When I started going to church, shortly after, I realized that he was literally sent by God! We both started going to church, got saved, and are still yoked together to this day. I can honestly tell you that we are beyond blessed because we are doing it God's way. We don't all start on the same path nor at the same time, but when we make up in our minds to do what's right, we can end up on the same path. Trust God!! He knows what we need and who to bring along the way. Our soul mate will be the one who will adhere to the vows and keep them!

◆◆◆ Day 20 ◆◆◆

Scripture of the Day!!

Romans 12:2 – *"And be not conformed to this world: but be ye transformed by the renewing of your mind, that ye may prove what is that good, and acceptable, and perfect, will of God."*

Questions of the Day!!

Are you still trying to fit in with this world?

_____
_____
_____
_____
_____
_____

Is your mind contaminated or renewed in Christ?

_____
_____

_____

_____

_____

_____

Inspiration of the Day!!

God wants us to have a do-right mind. Having a do-right mind requires us to renew our minds daily. It requires us to separate ourselves from the things we were once delivered from. It also requires us to pull on God for strength to fight against our weaknesses and demons that we are fighting. Sometimes in life, different circumstances can alter or influence our minds to convert us back to who we used to be and do what we used to do. That is why we must renew our minds daily.

When our minds have been contaminated, it's almost like having an infection. We all know what infections do. They spread! Sometimes it's easier to convert back to old things because it doesn't take much effort to do wrong. Let me help you! Transforming our minds is going to require effort on our part. We have to want it and put in the effort to make a change. Some things that we have carried from our youth into adulthood have been embedded in us, so it will be a battle between your flesh and emotions, but we can make it if we want it. It will not be easy to lay that thing down that we struggled with from youth, but transformation is ours for the asking. Remember, we must first make a choice, and then we will act upon our choice. Below are a few actions and adjectives using the letters in the word transformation to encourage you in some of the things you must partake in before and during transformation…...

- ✓ Trust God
- ✓ Rest in Him
- ✓ Adequate amount of God's teaching
- ✓ Nurture your spiritual being
- ✓ Surrender to God completely
- ✓ Foundation built on God
- ✓ Observant to the spirit of god
- ✓ Righteous in the eyes of the Lord
- ✓ Morally clean
- ✓ Accessible to do God's will
- ✓ Teachable to God's Word
- ✓ Inspire to be more like Christ
- ✓ Open to change
- ✓ Nourishing demeanor

The Love That You Need

Day 21

Scripture of the Day!!

Acts 2:17 – "And it shall come to pass in the last days, saith God, I will pour out my spirit upon all flesh: and your sons and your daughters shall prophesy, and your young men shall see visions, and your old men shall dream dreams."

Questions of the Day!!

Are you experiencing things that are hard to express to others?

_____

_____

_____

_____

_____

Are you struggling with accepting who you are?

_____

_____

_____

_____

_____

Inspiration of the Day!!

Growing up, I always knew that I was different. I would sometimes know things would happen beforehand, sense (discern) things, and I would always visit churches by myself. I'm talking about around the age of 14! I thought it was strange that I desired something/someone I did not know until I started to really understand, and I accepted salvation in my early 20's. Some of the things that I have experienced, I somewhat felt like why talk about it when people are not going to understand fully or think I am crazy.

In all honesty, I sometimes feel like that to this day. I had to realize that God calls whom He chooses, and I had to accept that I was His chosen vessel. He anointed me for such a time as this, and even though I didn't understand, I finally gave in and gave Him a yes. I must admit I ran for years because I didn't understand, and I didn't want to commit to something that I wasn't sure if I could hold up my end of the bargain.

Many of you are running from God like I did because of fear, misunderstanding, not wanting to submit, not wanting to surrender things that are not right, etc., but whatever it is, I want to encourage you to embrace who you are and accept you are different. Whatever you need, whether it be physically, spiritually, financially, emotionally, etc., allow God to fill that void. In due time it will all make sense when you give God a complete yes.

Testimonial......

I have dreams and visions almost every day! My very first dream that came to pass was in May 2007. I still remember vividly what took place, and not even a week later, my dream came to pass. I remember sitting there going over what I saw over and over again in amazement. I also found myself going to people trying to get answers that only God could give me. God spoke to me one day and said, seek me! I am the one that is revealing what's to come and what's going on right now. They can't help you because they don't know.

I had to repent, and after I repented, I started seeking Him (God) day in and day out for clarity and understanding. I want to give you a little insight into some of the things I have seen! God has revealed to me people in the bed committing fornication, people talking about me in the privacy of their own home, death before it happens, warnings about sheep in wolves' clothing, motives/intents of people's hearts, and so much more.

I really can't express the bulk of the visions/dreams to you because of limited space but just know you are special in God's eyes. God doesn't use everybody to reveal His secrets. Count it all joy and rest in Him, knowing that what He started in you, He will complete it. Often, it can be a little scary to see things and warn the people, but it is bearable. As you fulfill your purpose, God will grace you with what you need to push on. Give God a complete yes and allow Him to use you in the capacity you were created to be used. Somebody is waiting on your obedience to God so that you can reveal to them what the Lord is saying.

◆◆◆ Day 22 ◆◆◆

Scripture of the Day!!

1 Corinthians 7:14 – *"For the unbelieving husband is sanctified by the wife, and the unbelieving wife is sanctified by the husband: else were your children unclean; but now are they holy."*

Questions of the Day!!

What does your spouse see when he/she looks at you?

_____
_____
_____
_____
_____
_____

Are you a safe place for your spouse?

_____
_____

_____

_____

_____

_____

Inspiration of the Day!!

Marriage is definitely for the mature! Being married 18 years and together for 23, I can honestly say this scripture has helped me through the years. Early in our marriage, we made a vow that the big "D" word (divorce) would not be an option in our marriage. That gave us the mindset that whatever we face in our marriage had to be worked out. Being married is like having a job, and you must put your time in to make it work. It has been such a joy being married, and having a happy marriage makes it even better.

We must first remember that happiness starts within, and then it can exude outward. As a sanctified wife, I had to humble myself and seek God for wisdom to make my marriage work. First, I had to do some serious soul searching and allow God to perform spiritual surgery on me so that I wouldn't bleed on my husband and children. I had to humble myself and realize that every response doesn't require an answer and that every battle is not meant for me to fight. Even with being right, one must learn humility and have the mindset of never feeling the need to prove yourself. It's a must. If we want to see a change in our spouses, the change sometimes has to begin with us.

There were times when I went to God ready to give up, times I cried myself to sleep, times where I wanted to speak my mind, but Exodus 14:14 says the Lord shall fight for us, and we shall hold our peace. Never allow pride to overtake you and ruin what God has destined to be together and grow into something beautiful. We must remain steadfast, live the life God has graced us with in front of our mates, be forgiving, love hard, and always be willing to go above and beyond to make your marriage work.

Remember, we can't show our mates anything other than Christ if we want to win them over, so crucifying our flesh is a must. We have to do away with the cussing, degrading, immaturity, needing the last word syndrome, etc., and seek God's face for help.

Testimonial......

My daughter, Amanti's god sister, wrote a book titled *A Praying Wife*, and during the time she released her book, I was going through some pretty rough things in my marriage. I remember her godmother bringing the book to my house so I could read it and get more insight on how to be a wife and a wife of prayer. In this book, I found some interesting things that I took personally and started implementing them in my own marriage. May I add that shortly after then, my marriage started getting stronger.

Some might find it strange, but it definitely worked for me. I first started anointing my doors with oil. I then began to put anointing oil (extra virgin olive oil) into his body wash, lotion, rubbed it on his soap, on his deodorant, and even started cooking with it. When he would go to sleep at night, I would anoint his head with oil and his side of the bed. Was it an easy task at first? No! Did it get worse before it got better? It seemed that way at first, but the results I see today were well worth what I had to endure.

When you pray, study your word, and incorporate the tools that God has put in His word, it will turn into a success story every time if it's in the will of God.

Day 23

Scripture of the Day!!

James 1:8 – *"A double-minded man is unstable in all of his ways."*

Questions of the Day!!

Are you ready to be stable?

_____
_____
_____
_____
_____

Are you ready to be made whole?

_____
_____
_____

_____

_____

_____

Inspiration of the Day!!

When we are unstable, it's almost like we are divided between the world and God. Have you ever been to a circus and seen an acrobat trying to balance himself/herself on a rope and moving from side to side trying to keep their balance? That is what I visualized when studying the word unstable. Are you still wondering what the meaning of being unstable means? Unstable is another term used for unsafe, unreliable, or insecure, to name just a few. Being unstable can cause us to believe that we are doing right when in actuality, we are doing wrong. It causes us to be confused.

God's word states that He is not the author of confusion, so wherever confusion is present, God is absent. Instability comes upon us when we neglect to seek God for guidance and direction for our lives. God desires us to be stable, sober-minded, hearers and doers of His word, obedient, and so much more. As I was studying this scripture, what came to mind was "Functional Christians" – people who learn how to be practical, useful, and working but don't possess or carry the anointing or oil from God.

Again, that's not how God intended for us to be. We have to put forth the effort every day to be better than the day before. We have to fully submit our brokenness, our past, our future, and everything in between to give God the full range of our lives. He should always have full access to our heart, mind, body, and soul.

On today, let's focus on being whole and releasing everything that has us bound! Let's focus on being stable so we can have a sober mind! You can also write personal things that you need God to release you from on the lines below.

Affirmation……

Lord, we release everything that is causing us to be unstable and broken!! Death and life are in the power of our tongue, so………

- ✓ We release childhood pain/trauma
- ✓ We release molestation and rape
- ✓ We release abuse (mentally, physically, verbally)
- ✓ We release generational curses
- ✓ We release our fleshly desires
- ✓ We release our way
- ✓ We release our vain thoughts
- ✓ We release our disobedience
- ✓ We release our selfishness
- ✓ We release doubt and fear

- ✓ We release control
- ✓ We release our entire being to You
- ✓ _____
- ✓ _____
- ✓ _____
- ✓ _____
- ✓ _____
- ✓ _____

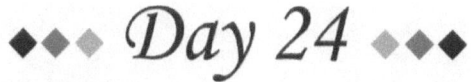

Day 24

Scripture of the Day!!

1 Samuel 15:22 – "And Samuel said, Hath the Lord as great delight in burnt offerings and sacrifices, as in obeying the voice of the Lord? Behold, to **obey is better than sacrifice**, and to hearken than the fat of rams......"

Questions of the Day!!

Do you listen and move in God more than you obey the desires of this world?

_____
_____
_____
_____
_____

Are you offering God your obedience, your sacrifices, or both?

_____

_____

_____

_____

_____

Inspiration of the Day!!

Learning to obey the voice of the Lord is crucial to being obedient. If we can't hear the voice of the Lord, it is impossible to obey Him. What is obedience? Obedience is submission to another's authority. Walking in obedience has major perks, but it can also be challenging at times. Remember, even in challenging times, we still must put forth the effort to obey. Offering up sacrifices to God is great when He requires the sacrifice.

I'm reminded that God sacrificed His only son to save us from sin, Mary sacrificed her reputation to birth Jesus, and Abraham took his son Isaac to the mount to be a sacrifice. They were all mandated by God! We have to be wise and strategic, so we can be in a place where we can discern the voice of the Lord, hearken unto His voice, and obey and follow. When we learn to obey, every promise in His word belongs to us. We can walk in assurance, knowing that every promise will be fulfilled in our lives, and every word spoken shall come to pass. Move in obedience to God no matter what it may cost. When you are doing a work for God, look to be ridiculed, have your name slandered, lies told on you, being misunderstood, being despitefully used, etc. Still, one thing remains the same; OBEDIENCE IS BETTER THAN SACRIFICE!!

Dream......

I was ready to throw in the towel because I was going through so much at the time, and I felt as if I was all alone. I remember falling to sleep and telling myself I'm over it all. God showed me in a dream how my life would in up if I went back into the world. I saw so many flashing lights (police cars), my sons being arrested, my household out of order, and so much more. Nevertheless, when I woke up, I repented, and I am still saved to this day. Obedience or disobedience all comes with a price that you will have to pay eventually. The price I want to pay is I want a reward afterward for being obedient.

Day 25

Scripture of the Day!!

Psalm 34:18 – *"The Lord is nigh unto them that are of a broken heart; and saveth such as a contrite spirit."*

Questions of the Day!!

Has your heart ever been broken? Provide an example.

_____
_____
_____
_____
_____

In your time of brokenness, who did you find yourself dependent upon?

_____
_____

Inspiration of the Day!!

When we operate or live our everyday lives in brokenness, we almost take on a prison-like mindset and become hostage in our own bodies. Our emotions start to speak before our mouths actually open, which could cause some serious danger. We become defensive, bitter, abusive, and close-minded.

In relationships, it's hard to trust and love because we always find ourselves reverting back to our past. One starts to shut down, isolate themselves, put up a wall of comfort, and the next step is a failed relationship. Some of us walk around every day on our jobs, in school, in our homes, etc., and don't even realize that we are broken. We are literally a walking time bomb. Be honest with yourself! What has happened to you that has caused you to be broken? It may be multiple things, but God can handle them all.

Don't be deceived! Brokenness can take form in many ways, such as anxiety, emptiness, bitterness, depression, shame, addictions, sex, alcohol, drugs, materialistic things, and so on. What comes to mind are innocent children. If you give them a puzzle and give them all of the pieces and they accidentally lose one, what do you think will happen next. I believe they will either color the spot where the missing piece goes or put something there that doesn't fit.

That is what we do in our brokenness. In reality, nothing can feel one's void but God. He is the only one that can take broken pieces and make them back whole. It is imperative that we draw nigh to God because, in His word, He promised that He is nigh unto them that are of a broken heart. Drawing nigh to God will allow us to heal properly! Once we heal properly, relationships will be restored, trust will be restored, and we will be able to love effectively. Acknowledgment is the first step to healing. As women, we learn how to function in the midst of our brokenness, but that is not how God designed us to function. Our desire today is, Lord, take us from brokenness to wholeness in You! It may not happen overnight, but we trust You, Lord, to do it.

Testimonial......

God spoke this to me during a women's conference! I had to teach a session on brokenness, and as I consecrated myself and studied, this is what He spoke to me.

- **Awareness** – Acknowledge that you are broken...... Denial will delay deliverance.
- **Know Your Worth** – Even though something/someone or maybe oneself has caused brokenness get up from that place of feeling sorry for

yourself and embrace your personal value. **Embrace who God made you.**

- **Forgiveness –** Let go of everything that is causing you to stay in that broken state. Forgive yourself and forgive others.

Everything We Need Is In God!

◆◆◆ Day 26 ◆◆◆

Scripture of the Day!!

Ephesians 6:1-3 – *"Children, obey your parents in the Lord: for this is right. Honor thy father and mother; (which is the first commandment with promise;) That it may be well with thee, and thou mayest live long on the earth."*

Questions of the Day!!

Are you honoring your parents in the capacity that God commanded you?

_____

_____

_____

_____

_____

Are your days extended or shortened because of the way you treat your parents?

_____

_____

_____

_____

_____

Inspiration of the Day!!

In society, we see all types of parenting. It sometimes breaks my heart because mostly what we see is babies raising babies with no experience or no one to guide them in parenting. When we step out there in the real world, we see so many children stealing, gangbanging, getting murdered, being disrespectful, having children, and so on. We must grab hold of our children and teach them the ways of the Lord. We must instill in them from their youth the word of God so that it can be embedded in them.

Are children perfect? No! Are we perfect? No! Will they get weak and fall sometimes? Yes! As long as you instill the word of the Lord, the Bible declares that one plants and one waters. What does that mean? As long as the word has been planted, someone will always come around to reiterate what has been taught. Disagreements will occur because we are all human and have different views on life, but we should be able to come together and come to a mutual agreement.

Ephesians 6 teaches us to obey our parents in the Lord! Sometimes we may not agree with everything they say or do, but respect should be the top priority. God's promise to us is that if we honor them, we will have longevity. Honoring our parents will cause God to move on our behalf because we are adhering to His word. We will live long on this earth! We all can be highly opinionated at times, but allowing your days to be shortened on earth to get the point across and to dishonor your parents is disgraceful. I want to live so I can see my great-great-great-grandchildren.

I want to encourage parents to know when you raise your children in the Lord, they may try you, but they know how far to go. Even in their adulthood, they will still honor you and give you the respect you deserve because of how you raised them.

Testimonial......

My husband and I have seven children with six living. One was born stillborn that we still count, but out of the six living, five are over the age of 18. There have been some days where I thought I had the best kids on this side of heaven, and then there are days when I question who my husband and I have raised. Children are not perfect, and neither were we growing up. I have learned whether our children want to hear the truth or not, we still have to teach them what the word of the Lord says. When we plant God's word in our children's lives, it will take root and grow over the years. They may look like they are getting away, but the fervent prayers of the righteous availeth much so we have to keep that prayer wheel turning. We can't throw our children away or try to live their lives because that is not the way God intended for it to be. Showing love is one of the things God repeatedly tells us in His word, and one verse that stands out to me says it's by loving-kindness that He has drawn all men to Him. What we instill in our children in their youth will definitely spring forth in their adult years.

My husband and I have three girls; two are in college and working, and one is still in high school. We have three sons; two work at good jobs, and one is in the military. Can I submit that when you put the fear of God in them and teach them the ways of the Lord, it will be a blessing to them and you in the long run? Don't be your children's friend. Parenting must come first!

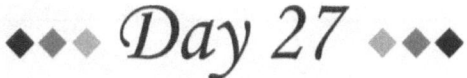

Scripture of the Day!!

Psalms 1:1-3 – "Blessed is the man that walketh not in the counsel of the ungodly, nor standeth in the way of sinners, nor sitteth in the seat of the scornful. But his delight is in the law of the Lord; and in his law doth he meditates day and night. And he shall be like a tree planted by the rivers of water, that bringeth forth his fruit in his season; his leaf shall not wither; and whatsoever he doeth shall prosper."

Questions of the Day!!

Are you planted around the right people and in the right place?

_____

_____

_____

_____

_____

What kind of fruit are you producing? Is it ripe or rotten?

_____

_____

_____

_____

_____

Inspiration of the Day!!

Most of us desire to be blessed in life, but we don't know what road we must take to get there. We want all the blessings of the Lord, but we sometimes lack in being obedient and faithful to God's word. This scripture took me back to my young adult days. I wanted to desperately hear from God and receive the many blessings spoken over my life and in God's word. I didn't start seeing the full manifestation of God's word until I got sick and tired of living the same old sinful life. I found myself trying to seek direction from sinners (the ungodly) and always found myself going in circles doing the very thing I was trying to get away from. In my time of need, I knew that the only person that could help me was the Lord.

We must turn from hanging with the ungodly, stop traveling down a sinful road, and stop following wicked advice. We must make a wise choice to follow the instructions of the Lord. When we align with God's plan and His word, whatever we do will be blessed. We must stay in God's word and be a hearer as well as a doer so that transformation will take place. I am reminded of a saying I used to hear when I first received Christ. Below you will find a few ways to be blessed and stay blessed. You can add your own from the word!

- Be careful little ears what you hear
- Be careful little eyes what you see
- Be careful little mouth what you say

Affirmations to Be Blessed......

- Be in Christ/Christ in you

Ephesians 1:3

- Keep God's Commandments

Exodus 20:6

- Honor/Respect your parents

Exodus 20:12

- Ask God for it

James 4:2

- Be a blessing to others

Proverbs 11:25

- Repent

Acts 3:19

- _____
- _____
- _____
- _____
- _____
- _____
- _____
- _____

Day 28

Scripture of the Day!!

Habakkuk 2:3 – *"For the vision is yet for an appointed time, but at the end it shall speak, and not lie: though it tarry, wait for it; because it will surely come, it will not tarry."*

Questions of the Day!!

What are you waiting on God to do that has already been revealed to you?

_____

_____

_____

_____

_____

In your tarrying season, are you trusting God in your wait?

_____

_____

_____

_____

_____

_____

Inspiration of the Day!!

We all have things that we are believing God for. Sometimes God even gives us a small glimpse of where He is taking us, and we get so anxious because we want to be in that place now. A lot of us find ourselves getting weary because things are not happening when we want them to. In our waiting season, we have to do just what the word says, wait. God's timing is not our timing, but His timing is the right time. What God has promised shall come to pass, and it will speak for itself. We sometimes have to step back and ask ourselves, one, are we ready to receive what we are praying for, two, will we appreciate what we are praying for if God releases it, and three are we mentally and emotionally stable to handle what comes with what we are praying for?

Sometimes even lack of maturity will cause our visions and prayers to tarry. No matter how long you are in your waiting season, keep the faith and don't give up. We all have waited on God in some way! Waiting doesn't always feel good when what you are seeking God for seems to be urgent in your eyes. In reality, God is not slack of His promise and what He said He will do. Keep believing, keep trusting, keep relying on God to fulfill His purpose and plan even in your waiting season. Sometimes when we have to wait, it seems like God is not near, but in my waiting season, I learned to ask God when I can't trace You, help me to trust You.

Vision......

I was in a grocery store talking to this young woman while she was stocking groceries on different shelves. After discussing various things, I ended up in my bedroom talking to one of my daughters. She began to look at me with this look of embarrassment, so I asked her what was wrong. She nodded her head nothing, but it was revealed to me that she was pregnant. I asked her if she was pregnant, and she said yes, so then I asked if she was going to keep it, and she said yes. I began to encourage her, and then we ended up in my living room. Three of my children were in the family room talking to my husband, and as I came down the stairs, my husband was in the recliner. He was talking to the children, and as I looked at my daughter, she had the same look on her face as before. My husband asked her what was wrong, and she asked me to tell him she was pregnant. In the midst of the conversation in the vision, it was said that I had three grandchildren on the way by three different children.

When I woke up, I immediately started praying because I felt a little overwhelmed, thinking three of my children were expecting. In the midst of me praying, the Father, the Son, and the Holy Ghost kept coming out of my mouth. As I began to listen to the voice of the Lord, He said everything that I have spoken has to conform to my word. He then took me to the book of Genesis when He spoke creation and form to this world. The number three was very significant to this vision and the pregnancy. Even when carrying a child, you have to wait nine months before delivery. Still, during your waiting months, the unborn fetus is conforming (adapting/adjusting), so when the delivery time comes, he/she will be complete and healthy.

Before God gave me this vision, we were in the process of purchasing a home. The third home we bid on is the home we are closing on. We were approved for 300,000 to purchase a home. We have a 3% interest rate. We rented three houses before we purchased this home. Again, in your waiting time, be patient and don't make premature decisions. If God said it would happen in His timing, I promise you it will be well worth the wait!

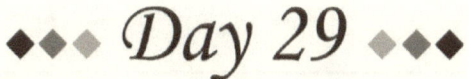

Scripture of the Day!!

Colossians 3:23-25 – *"And whatsoever ye do, do it heartily, as to the Lord, and not unto men; Knowing that of the Lord ye shall receive the reward of the inheritance: for ye serve the Lord Christ. But he that doeth wrong shall receive for the wrong which he hath done: and there is no respect of persons."*

Questions of the Day!!

Have you ever felt unappreciated after giving your all?

_____
_____
_____
_____
_____
_____

Have you ever felt overlooked for something you know you were called to do?

_____

_____

_____

_____

_____

Inspiration of the Day!!

I am reminded of David (Jesse's son) when Saul was looking to anoint the next king. Can you put yourself in his shoes and imagine the emotions that he was feeling? David was overlooked, but he was the chosen one!

This situation reminds me of what many of us find ourselves in every day. We have been overlooked for positions on our jobs, working in the ministry, relationships, etc., but that still didn't disqualify us from being called out or chosen by God. Often, we are overlooked because of jealousy, intimidation, and lack of identity in ourselves, but we must stand steadfast and unmovable.

Looking back over my life, I remember being looked over and not even acknowledged as a Missionary in the church. I would go home and cry and vent to my husband because of the pain it caused me. I had to conclude that the Lord chose me and anointed me to be who I am. Whether man overlooked me or didn't appreciate me, I still had to move according to God's word, and whatever I did, I had to do it wholeheartedly as unto God. It wasn't an easy task, but with God, all things are possible. Also, our reward comes from God, and I would rather hear Him say, well done thy good and faithful servant than to please man any day.

Testimonial......

For a long time, I felt complacent in my walk with Christ. The reason being is because I was so concerned about what people think about me. The funny thing is God revealed to me who I was in Him but where I was physically and spiritually was a struggle. Why was it a struggle? I struggled because I was scared of what I was experiencing, and I felt no one would understand. Seeing things before they happen, experiencing the supernatural, hearing private conversations, etc., was strange to me. Keep in mind I didn't come from a family that knew God, so I felt like a tree in the desert. The time I did ask someone (leaders) about what I was experiencing, their response was so discouraging it made me second guess myself. The discouragement caused me to fall back into the spirit of being complacent because of a lack of understanding.

One day the Lord spoke to me in a vision and asked me why do I keep going to people that don't understand the call that's on my life. I am the creator of your being, and I know exactly what you are going through. He told me to seek Him for what I need! I have been doing that ever since, and I feel myself getting stronger by the day. Man can't fully understand something that they are not anointed to operate in. Seek God, study His word, pray, and then stop to listen to see what the Lord is saying to you. Why not seek the maker, the creator, the redeemer, the all-wise, and all-knowing one who will definitely lead us into all truth?

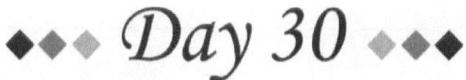

Scripture of the Day!!

Romans 10:13 – *"For whosoever shall call upon the name of the Lord shall be saved…"*

Questions of the Day!!

Whose name are you calling upon in your time of trouble?

_____
_____
_____
_____
_____
_____

What/Whose help are you reaching out for?

_____
_____
_____

_____

_____

_____

Inspiration of the Day!!

In life, we will endure joy, sorrow, grief, happiness, sadness, ups and downs, and so on. Life is meant for us to live in abundance! Even in our weakest and most trying moments, we can call on the Lord for help, and He will be right there. So many times in life, we fall because we don't know who to turn to or whose name to call upon. It is okay to call mommy and daddy, sister and brother, pastor, first lady, and even friends, but can they meet the need that we have at the moment. Can they offer the genuine help that we are seeking? I'm not saying talking to people is wrong. All I am saying is know when it should be a God conversation versus a people conversation. We must know the difference!

This scripture encourages us to call upon the name of the Lord. Everyone who cries out, "Help, God," will receive help. To call for help, we must first trust God, and to trust God, we must know Him for ourselves. I realize personally that we must be willing to take the time and put forth the effort to know God. In your season of plentifulness and your season of lack, in your season of mourning and your season of joy, in your season of sowing, and in your season of reaping, call on the name of the Lord for help. You don't have to face anything alone. Call on the Lord and allow Him to help you every step of the way. He is there with arms stretched wide open to help.

Testimonial......

Being raised in a project from the age of 4 to 14 wasn't easy. Growing up, I was taught and learned some bad habits that were hard to break when I received Christ. See, a lot of people view things differently but when you find yourself in a tough situation truth is you don't know what you would do or how you will react.

Growing up, I was taught/learned to fight (to defend myself by any means necessary), cuss people, don't take any mess from NOBODY, etc. I have always been a quiet person, but the ones who know me know I didn't back down from a challenge. I remember cussing a police officer out to his face because he made me upset, and I could have gone to jail for being rude and nasty. I have been in fights and even been cut in my face under my eye (barely missed my eye) and still kept going. I have even been locked outside the door to fight because I was chased home, and my mother wasn't having it.

As I grew in Christ, I had to learn how to constantly call upon the name of the Lord. I learned that God is my safe place, He is my redeemer, He is the one that regulates my mind, He is my strength, He is my all and all, and when I am in need, He is my help, He is my everything.

For years I wondered how I was going to serve God being the way that I was. I remember thinking, Lord, how am I going to serve You, and my temper is bad when I get upset. My mouth cuts people skin deep. I don't take foolishness from people. I will fight at the drop of a dime, etc. but God. When we call on the name of the Lord and are sincere, the transformation will take place. If we really want it, it's ours for the asking.

I want to encourage you, yes, you, the one who is reading this. YOU DON'T HAVE TO STAY THE WAY YOU ARE! God is just a call away. You don't even need a telephone; all you have to do is open your mouth and call upon Him, and He will answer. The good thing is what you tell Him, you will never hear it again!

Notes!!!!!

Notes!!!!!

www.ingramcontent.com/pod-product-compliance
Lightning Source LLC
Chambersburg PA
CBHW030911080526
44589CB00010B/246